Nvidia's NVM 1.0
AI's Next Frontier – What's It All About?

A Deep Dive into the Model That's Reshaping Technology, Research, and Innovation

Jackson Z. Scott

Table of Contents

Introduction

Nvidia has long been synonymous with technological breakthroughs, carving a niche as a pioneer in artificial intelligence and computing innovation. From revolutionizing GPU technology to becoming a cornerstone for AI training and deployment, Nvidia has consistently pushed the limits of what technology can achieve. Its reputation as a leader in the field isn't just built on hardware excellence but also on its ability to anticipate the needs of an ever-evolving industry, offering solutions that transform how we interact with machines.

With the introduction of NVM 1.0, Nvidia has once again disrupted the landscape. This new model represents more than just an incremental step forward; it signals a paradigm shift in the capabilities of artificial intelligence. Multimodal AI—once thought of as a challenge too complex to master—has found its champion in NVM 1.0. This model isn't merely designed to process tasks in isolation; it seamlessly integrates vision and language capabilities to tackle real-world problems in ways that were previously unimaginable. Whether it's analyzing complex images, understanding context, solving intricate mathematical problems, or even decoding humor, NVM 1.0 has redefined what it means to be a generalist AI with specialist-level precision.

What makes this model truly groundbreaking isn't just its multimodal functionality but its ability to excel in text-based tasks as well—a domain where many similar systems falter. It bridges a critical gap by demonstrating dual strength, showing that an AI can master vision and text simultaneously without compromise. Even more impressive is Nvidia's commitment to democratizing access to this innovation. By making the model's weights and training code freely available, they have invited the global AI community to build on this foundation, sparking collaboration and accelerating progress across industries.

The purpose of this book is to dive deeply into the transformative nature of NVM 1.0. Through its pages, we will explore not only the technical brilliance of the model but also the profound impact it promises to have on research, technology, and society at large. This is a story of innovation, vision, and the relentless pursuit of excellence—a story that reflects the very ethos Nvidia embodies. With NVM 1.0, the future of AI isn't just closer than we imagined; it's unfolding before our eyes.

Chapter 1: The Birth of NVM 1.0

Nvidia's journey as a trailblazer in artificial intelligence can be traced back to its inception, where it began as a leader in graphics processing units (GPUs). What initially started as a quest to revolutionize gaming and visual computing quickly evolved into something much larger. Nvidia's GPUs, designed for high-performance parallel computing, became the backbone of modern AI development, enabling researchers to process massive datasets and train complex neural networks at unprecedented speeds.

The turning point came when Nvidia shifted its focus toward making AI accessible not just for academics but for industries and developers around the world. With the release of CUDA, a groundbreaking parallel computing platform, Nvidia opened the door for programmers to harness GPU power in ways that were previously unimaginable. This innovation fueled the rise of deep learning, enabling breakthroughs in areas like image recognition, natural language processing, and autonomous systems.

Nvidia's track record in AI innovation is marked by key milestones, from powering AlphaGo—the first AI to defeat a human world champion in the ancient game of Go—to the development of DGX systems, which became the gold standard for AI infrastructure. The company also played a pivotal role in advancing autonomous vehicles, robotics, and healthcare, providing the computational muscle behind applications that depend on real-time processing and intelligent decision-making.

The rise of multimodal AI was another significant chapter in Nvidia's legacy. As AI models grew more sophisticated, the need for systems that could seamlessly integrate different types of data—text, images, speech—became apparent. Nvidia anticipated this need and began laying the groundwork for what would eventually become NVM 1.0. The company's research into natural language understanding, computer vision, and cross-modal tasks culminated in a series of innovations that redefined the capabilities of AI.

NVM 1.0 is not just a product of this history; it's the embodiment of Nvidia's vision for the future. It builds on decades of expertise and a relentless drive to solve the industry's toughest challenges. By combining multimodal capabilities, groundbreaking architecture, and unparalleled performance, NVM 1.0 represents the next logical step in a journey defined by constant innovation. From GPUs to deep learning accelerators and now to multimodal intelligence, Nvidia's legacy is one of foresight, adaptation, and the ability to shape the trajectory of AI itself.

The advent of multimodal AI models brought a wave of excitement and possibilities, yet it also revealed a set of glaring limitations that needed addressing. These models, designed to process and interpret both text and visual inputs, often excelled in one domain while falling short in the other. For example, models built for vision-heavy tasks struggled to maintain high performance on text-based challenges, and vice versa. This trade-off meant that existing multimodal systems were either specialists in narrow tasks or lacked the flexibility to deliver consistent results across diverse applications.

Another significant challenge was the degradation in text-based accuracy during multimodal training. Many models, while integrating image and text processing capabilities, experienced a noticeable drop in their ability to perform well on benchmarks like coding, mathematical reasoning, or textual comprehension. This imbalance left researchers and industries with tools that were powerful in theory but often impractical for real-world applications requiring high precision and adaptability.

Moreover, the reliance on vast datasets to train these models introduced issues of scalability and diminishing returns. Simply increasing the size of the dataset without ensuring its quality often led to inefficiencies in training and suboptimal results. Multimodal AI was in desperate need of a new paradigm—one that could balance its capabilities without compromise, ensure consistent excellence across tasks, and prioritize meaningful data over sheer volume.

This is where Nvidia's NVM 1.0 comes into the picture. The model was built to address these challenges head-on, guided by three foundational principles: a hybrid architecture, a focus on high-quality data, and a solution to the trade-off problem that had plagued previous systems.

NVM 1.0's hybrid architecture is a marvel in itself. By combining the strengths of decoder-only models, known for their text-processing prowess, and cross-attention-based models, designed for vision-language integration, Nvidia created a system capable of excelling across modalities. This blend allows the model to harness the precision of text-dedicated frameworks while seamlessly integrating visual reasoning, resulting in unparalleled performance in both domains.

The second key innovation lies in the emphasis on quality over quantity in data selection. Nvidia curated a carefully balanced dataset designed to enhance specific capabilities. Instead of merely expanding the size of the training data, they incorporated diverse, high-quality text data alongside multimodal math and reasoning datasets. This strategic approach ensured that NVM 1.0 would not only process vast amounts of information but do so with a level of understanding and precision unmatched by its predecessors.

Finally, NVM 1.0 addresses the long-standing trade-off problem by enhancing both text and vision performance simultaneously. Unlike competing models that see a decline in one area when training for another, Nvidia engineered NVM 1.0 to excel in both. This was achieved through its innovative training methods and architectural design, which optimized the system to build on its strengths rather than compromise them.

The development of NVM 1.0 was not just about creating another AI model. It was a deliberate, groundbreaking effort to redefine what multimodal AI could achieve. By solving the core limitations of its predecessors and setting a new benchmark for performance, NVM 1.0 stands as a testament to Nvidia's commitment to pushing boundaries and meeting the demands of an evolving industry.

The concept of "dual strength" sits at the heart of what makes Nvidia's NVM 1.0 such a groundbreaking achievement in artificial intelligence. In the world of multimodal AI, dual strength refers to a model's ability to excel in two key domains simultaneously: vision-language integration and text-based reasoning. This balance has long been a challenge for AI developers, as most multimodal models tend to show strengths in one area while faltering in another. NVM 1.0 defies these constraints, redefining what it means to be a truly versatile AI.

Traditional multimodal models like GPT-4, Intern VL2, and Llama 3v have made significant strides in their respective areas, but each comes with its own set of trade-offs. GPT-4, widely regarded as a leader in text-based tasks, falls short when it comes to integrating vision and language tasks effectively. While it excels in natural language understanding and reasoning, its ability to process and analyze visual data remains limited, leaving room for improvement in tasks that require seamless multimodal comprehension.

Intern VL2, on the other hand, was designed with vision-language tasks in mind, positioning itself as a robust contender for visual reasoning challenges. However, its strength in multimodal performance comes at a cost—degradation in text-based capabilities. Models like Intern VL2 often struggle to maintain high accuracy on textual reasoning tasks after being trained for multimodal use, which limits their utility in applications requiring advanced language processing, such as coding or complex mathematical reasoning.

Llama 3v, a highly anticipated model, attempted to address the trade-off problem by freezing its text-processing backbone during multimodal training. While this approach preserved its performance on text-heavy tasks, it limited the model's ability to grow and evolve across modalities. This lack of simultaneous improvement in both text and vision tasks highlights a fundamental limitation in its design.

NVM 1.0 sets itself apart by overcoming these barriers. Nvidia engineered the model to enhance both vision-language tasks and text-based reasoning simultaneously, without sacrificing performance in either domain. This dual strength is a rare and valuable trait in the AI landscape, allowing NVM 1.0 to seamlessly handle tasks as diverse as optical character recognition (OCR), visual question answering (VQA), complex mathematical problem-solving, and precise text-based analysis.

What makes NVM 1.0's dual strength even more impressive is its consistency. While competitors struggle with degradation or limited growth in specific areas, NVM 1.0 demonstrates exceptional reliability across benchmarks. It outperforms GPT-4 in vision-language integration, matches or surpasses Intern VL2 in multimodal tasks, and exhibits growth that Llama 3v cannot achieve, thanks to its innovative training architecture and quality-focused dataset.

This ability to excel across modalities redefines the possibilities for multimodal AI. By erasing the trade-offs that have long hindered the field, NVM 1.0 is not just closing the gap between text and vision tasks—it's setting a new standard for what AI can accomplish. This dual strength is what positions it as a game changer, not just for researchers and developers but for industries that depend on AI to solve real-world challenges with precision and versatility.

Chapter 2: Understanding Multimodal AI

Multimodal AI refers to a class of artificial intelligence systems designed to process and integrate multiple types of data, such as text and visual inputs, to perform tasks that require an understanding of both formats simultaneously. Unlike traditional AI models that specialize in one domain—either text or images—multimodal models aim to bridge the gap between these formats, enabling them to interpret, reason, and make decisions in ways that mimic human cognitive abilities. This capability opens the door to a wide range of applications, from interpreting complex visual data to generating coherent, contextually rich textual responses based on visual stimuli.

At the core of multimodal AI lies its ability to combine and cross-reference information from different data modalities. For instance, a multimodal model can analyze an image of a receipt and extract text-based details, such as the total amount or item descriptions, while simultaneously understanding the visual structure of the document. This seamless integration of vision and language enables the model to excel at tasks that require both formats to work in harmony, such as optical character recognition (OCR), visual question answering (VQA), and reasoning through complex scenarios.

What makes multimodal AI revolutionary is its potential to solve problems that are beyond the reach of single-modal systems. In the real world, information rarely exists in isolation; images often come with textual descriptions, and text frequently refers to visual elements. The ability to process these modalities together mirrors the way humans interpret the world, making multimodal AI a critical step toward creating systems that can think and act more holistically.

This breakthrough is particularly significant in industries where the ability to understand both text and visuals is essential. For example, in healthcare, multimodal AI can analyze medical images alongside patient records to provide more accurate diagnoses. In education, it can power interactive tools that teach students through a combination of diagrams, text, and contextual explanations. Even in fields like content creation, multimodal models can analyze visual trends and generate corresponding narratives, bridging the gap between human creativity and machine intelligence.

The revolutionary nature of excelling at tasks that require an understanding of both text and visuals becomes even clearer when considering the limitations of previous systems. Traditionally, AI models designed for text lacked the ability to process visual data, and vice versa. This division created inefficiencies and limited the scope of what AI could achieve. By integrating these capabilities, multimodal models like Nvidia's NVM 1.0 unlock entirely new possibilities, from generating insights across diverse datasets to enabling more intuitive human-computer interactions.

In short, multimodal AI doesn't just represent an incremental improvement—it marks a paradigm shift in how we think about artificial intelligence. By empowering machines to understand and interpret the complexities of a multimodal world, these systems redefine the boundaries of what AI can achieve and open the door to innovations that once seemed far beyond reach.

Nvidia's NVM 1.0 stands out in the crowded field of multimodal AI by not just competing with, but often surpassing, its peers in both capability and performance. Unlike many of its competitors, which excel in isolated domains or specific benchmarks, NVM 1.0 demonstrates consistent excellence across a wide array of tasks, making it one of the most versatile and powerful models to date.

Take, for instance, the domain of optical character recognition (OCR), where many AI models struggle to balance precision and adaptability. NVM 1.0 excels not only at recognizing text embedded in images but also at understanding the context behind the text. This ability allows it to analyze complex documents, extract critical information, and even summarize the content meaningfully. In practical applications, such as processing financial invoices or digitizing handwritten medical records, this level of performance isn't just helpful—it's transformative.

In the field of visual question answering (VQA), NVM 1.0 further cements its superiority. Models tasked with VQA often stumble when asked to reason about an image's visual elements in conjunction with textual inputs. For example, identifying a specific object in an image based on a nuanced query or interpreting charts and graphs with detailed follow-up questions can be challenging for traditional models. NVM 1.0 not only performs these tasks with state-of-the-art accuracy but also reasons dynamically, offering insights that are precise and context-aware. Imagine a user asking the model to analyze a scientific chart and then requesting an explanation of anomalies in the data—NVM 1.0 handles this seamlessly, a feat that few competitors can achieve with the same level of sophistication.

Reasoning-based tasks, particularly those involving complex math and coding, reveal another critical area where NVM 1.0 outshines its competition. Many multimodal models experience a decline in text-based reasoning accuracy after being trained to handle visual tasks. In contrast, NVM 1.0 not only avoids this degradation but actually improves performance in text-based domains, achieving a remarkable 4.3-point boost in benchmarks related to math and coding accuracy. This dual strength is what sets NVM 1.0 apart—it excels at solving intricate equations, analyzing handwritten pseudo-code, and providing step-by-step solutions with clarity and precision.

What truly distinguishes NVM 1.0 is its ability to perform consistently across all these domains. Competing models like GPT-4, while powerful in text-heavy tasks, falter when tasked with complex multimodal challenges. Similarly, Intern VL2 may excel in vision-language tasks but struggles with text-centric reasoning. Even Llama 3v, which attempts to preserve text-based performance during multimodal training, fails to achieve the kind of growth seen in NVM 1.0, as its architecture inherently limits its ability to enhance across modalities.

Nvidia's NVM 1.0 doesn't just meet the bar set by its competitors—it raises it. By achieving unparalleled results in OCR, VQA, and reasoning tasks, it demonstrates its versatility and positions itself as the go-to model for industries that require AI capable of tackling diverse, real-world problems. Whether it's automating processes in healthcare, providing insights in education, or empowering businesses with advanced document analysis, NVM 1.0 isn't just leading the race—it's redefining the finish line.

Nvidia's NVM 1.0 has made waves in the AI industry not only because of its versatility but also because of its benchmark performance, where it has consistently set new standards. To understand why this model is being hailed as a game-changer, one only needs to look at how it fares on critical benchmarks like OCR Bench, Math Vista, and Chart QA. These benchmarks serve as rigorous tests of an AI model's capability to handle complex multimodal tasks, and NVM 1.0 doesn't just perform well—it dominates.

OCR Bench is a benchmark that evaluates a model's ability to perform optical character recognition (OCR), a task that involves extracting and understanding text embedded in images. Many models can accurately recognize text, but few can grasp the surrounding context or handle complex layouts like scanned documents or handwritten notes. NVM 1.0 excels here by leveraging its innovative architecture and data training strategy. It doesn't stop at simply identifying text; it understands its meaning within the visual and structural context of the document. For example, when analyzing an invoice, NVM 1.0 can differentiate between headers, itemized lists, and totals, all while maintaining accuracy that surpasses previous state-of-the-art models.

Math Vista is where NVM 1.0's reasoning abilities shine. This benchmark assesses a model's capability to interpret and solve mathematical problems that often involve complex visual inputs, such as handwritten equations or charts. Many AI systems falter when visual data needs to be paired with logical reasoning, but NVM 1.0 demonstrates exceptional strength. It not only recognizes and processes visual information but also applies mathematical reasoning to derive correct answers. Whether it's solving equations written on a whiteboard or analyzing numerical trends in a graph, NVM 1.0 delivers accurate results with a precision that represents a 4.3-point improvement over competitors. This leap in performance underscores its ability to seamlessly integrate vision and reasoning, making it invaluable in educational and professional settings.

Chart QA evaluates a model's understanding of visual data in the form of graphs, charts, and other structured visualizations, coupled with its ability to answer detailed questions about that data. This is one of the most demanding benchmarks because it requires a model to interpret visual elements, recognize patterns, and provide contextually accurate answers in textual form. For instance, analyzing a line chart to identify trends, anomalies, or correlations requires not just visual recognition but reasoning and context-awareness. NVM 1.0 consistently outperforms its peers in this domain by not only delivering accurate responses but also explaining its reasoning clearly, something few models have managed to achieve with such consistency.

Across these benchmarks, what truly sets NVM 1.0 apart is its **consistency and balance**. Where other models tend to excel in one area while underperforming in others, NVM 1.0 delivers top-tier results across the board. Competing systems like GPT-4, Intern VL2, and Llama 3v show strengths in isolated domains but fail to match NVM 1.0's ability to handle text, visuals, and reasoning simultaneously. This consistency makes NVM 1.0 not just a powerful model but a versatile tool capable of solving real-world problems with unparalleled efficiency.

In an industry where benchmarks serve as a definitive measure of progress, NVM 1.0's results are a clear indication that it isn't just another AI model—it's a transformative leap forward. By excelling in OCR, Math Vista, and Chart QA, NVM 1.0 has proven that it has the strength, precision, and adaptability to lead the next generation of multimodal AI.

Chapter 3: Architecture and Training—The Foundation of Excellence

At the heart of NVM 1.0's groundbreaking capabilities is its hybrid architecture, a design that combines the strengths of two distinct yet complementary approaches: decoder-only models and cross-attention-based models. This innovative integration allows NVM 1.0 to achieve a level of performance that not only outclasses its predecessors but also addresses many of the fundamental challenges associated with multimodal AI systems.

Decoder-only models have long been celebrated for their proficiency in processing and generating text. They are structured to focus on the sequential relationships within textual data, excelling at tasks like language comprehension, text completion, and reasoning. These models are particularly effective for tasks that rely heavily on understanding context within text-based inputs, such as solving mathematical equations, generating coherent explanations, or providing detailed coding assistance. By leveraging this design, NVM 1.0 inherits a robust foundation for handling complex text-based reasoning tasks.

On the other hand, cross-attention-based models are optimized for integrating and processing multiple modalities, particularly text and images. These models use attention mechanisms to draw connections between different data formats, enabling them to identify relationships and contextual relevance across modalities. For example, in a task like visual question answering, a cross-attention-based model can align textual questions with specific elements in an image, making it highly effective in vision-language tasks.

By combining these two approaches, NVM 1.0 achieves what many other multimodal models could not: the ability to perform at a high level across both text and vision tasks without compromising on either. The hybrid architecture allows the model to capitalize on the strengths of decoder-only systems for precise text comprehension while using the cross-attention mechanism to seamlessly integrate visual and textual data for multimodal reasoning.

This architecture is particularly effective because it avoids the common trade-offs seen in other models. In many cases, training a model to handle vision-language tasks leads to a decline in its text-based performance, as resources are redirected to handle the additional complexity of multimodal integration. Conversely, models optimized for text often lack the structural capabilities needed to process and reason with visual data effectively. NVM 1.0 sidesteps this dilemma by ensuring that the two architectural components complement rather than compete with each other.

A practical example of this synergy can be seen in how NVM 1.0 handles high-resolution images alongside textual inputs. In tasks like document analysis, the decoder-only framework processes and contextualizes the textual information, while the cross-attention-based component identifies and reasons about visual elements. This dual processing ensures that the model provides accurate, contextually relevant insights, whether it's extracting text from an image, interpreting its layout, or answering questions about the content.

The hybrid architecture of NVM 1.0 isn't just a clever design choice—it's a solution to the longstanding challenges that have limited multimodal AI. By bridging the gap between text and vision tasks with a balanced, unified approach, NVM 1.0 sets a new standard for performance and adaptability, proving that AI can excel across domains without compromise.

One of the most innovative features of NVM 1.0 is its use of 1D Tile Tagging, a design choice that significantly enhances the model's ability to process high-resolution images with precision and efficiency. High-resolution images, such as scanned documents or detailed visual data, pose unique challenges for AI models. The sheer volume of information within these images often overwhelms standard processing architectures, leading to reduced accuracy or missed details in critical tasks like optical character recognition (OCR) and dynamic visual reasoning.

1D Tile Tagging tackles this issue head-on by breaking down high-resolution images into smaller, manageable "tiles." Instead of forcing the model to analyze an entire image at once, which can dilute its focus and computational resources, this method assigns each tile a specific "tag" that captures both its content and its spatial context within the larger image. This enables NVM 1.0 to process each tile independently while retaining an understanding of how each piece fits into the broader visual structure.

This approach offers several advantages. First, it allows the model to focus on fine-grained details without being overwhelmed by the size of the image. For instance, in a detailed document, the model can accurately identify text within a specific section while simultaneously understanding its position relative to headings, charts, or other visual elements. Second, 1D Tile Tagging ensures that high-resolution images can be processed efficiently without sacrificing speed or accuracy, making the model highly effective in applications such as document analysis, medical imaging, and technical drawings.

The true power of 1D Tile Tagging lies in its ability to combine detail-oriented precision with contextual awareness. Whether analyzing a densely packed financial report or interpreting complex visual data like engineering schematics, NVM 1.0 uses this innovative design to deliver results that are not only accurate but also contextually meaningful. This feature positions the model as an invaluable tool in industries where high-resolution image processing is a cornerstone of success.

In building NVM 1.0, Nvidia adopted a revolutionary approach to training data that prioritizes quality over sheer quantity. While many AI models are trained on massive datasets to maximize exposure to diverse information, this approach often leads to diminishing returns. Large datasets, if not carefully curated, can introduce noise, redundancy, and biases that dilute a model's overall performance. Nvidia recognized this limitation and took a meticulous, targeted approach to data selection for NVM 1.0.

Rather than simply expanding the size of its training datasets, Nvidia focused on ensuring the data was both diverse and high-quality. For text-based tasks, the team curated a refined dataset rich in contextually relevant, high-fidelity information. This dataset was designed to enhance the model's understanding of nuanced language, logical reasoning, and problem-solving, ensuring that NVM 1.0 could excel in tasks like coding, mathematical reasoning, and text comprehension.

In addition to its text dataset, Nvidia carefully integrated multimodal training data that combined visual and textual elements. This data wasn't just selected for its volume but for its ability to teach the model how to handle complex, real-world scenarios. Examples include high-resolution document scans, mathematical equations embedded in visual formats, and context-rich visual question answering tasks. The goal was to ensure that the model didn't just learn to process information but to reason and draw meaningful insights across modalities.

This quality-driven strategy produced results that speak for themselves. While many multimodal models experience performance trade-offs—excelling in one domain at the expense of another—NVM 1.0 demonstrates exceptional consistency across benchmarks. Its performance improvements, such as the 4.3-point boost in text-based tasks, are a direct result of Nvidia's focus on curating high-impact data rather than overwhelming the model with unnecessary volume.

By choosing quality over quantity, Nvidia has redefined how AI models are trained. The result is an AI system that isn't just powerful—it's precise, adaptable, and ready to solve real-world problems with unmatched efficiency. This meticulous data strategy ensures that NVM 1.0 isn't just versatile but also a model of excellence in every sense of the word.

One of Nvidia's most remarkable achievements with NVM 1.0 is how it managed to balance multimodal and text-based capabilities without sacrificing performance in either domain. This balance was not achieved by chance but through a series of carefully engineered innovations and a strategic approach to training efficiency. Nvidia's ability to overcome the long-standing trade-off problem—where excelling in one area often results in diminished performance in another—is a testament to its thoughtful and forward-thinking design principles.

The core of this balance lies in NVM 1.0's **hybrid architecture**, which integrates the strengths of decoder-only models for text and cross-attention-based models for vision-language tasks. Instead of treating these components as competing systems, Nvidia designed them to complement one another. During training, the model leverages the decoder's strength to handle intricate text-based tasks, such as coding and mathematical reasoning, while simultaneously employing cross-attention mechanisms to process and integrate visual data for tasks like OCR and visual question answering. This architectural synergy allows NVM 1.0 to enhance both modalities without compromising its ability to perform at a high level in either.

Another key to training efficiency was Nvidia's focus on **progressive optimization strategies**. By carefully structuring the training process, Nvidia avoided the pitfall of overloading the model with complex multimodal tasks too early. Instead, the training was designed to gradually integrate visual and textual data, ensuring the model could master each domain before combining them. This phased approach allowed NVM 1.0 to maintain its precision in text-based tasks while scaling its multimodal capabilities.

A significant factor in maintaining performance was Nvidia's use of **selectively curated, high-quality datasets**. As opposed to overburdening the model with enormous datasets that could introduce noise and inefficiencies, Nvidia focused on feeding NVM 1.0 clean, diverse, and contextually rich data. This meant the model wasn't wasting computational resources on redundant or irrelevant information, allowing it to learn more effectively. The text dataset was designed to enhance logical reasoning, coding, and problem-solving skills, while the multimodal dataset included scenarios that required a seamless understanding of text and visuals, such as analyzing charts or solving math problems presented in handwritten formats.

The innovation didn't stop at the data—it extended to the **training framework itself**. Nvidia employed a combination of multitask learning and fine-tuning techniques, optimizing the model for specific tasks while retaining its general capabilities. For instance, fine-tuning the model on high-priority benchmarks, such as OCR and coding, ensured that it could excel in specialized tasks without losing its broader utility. This multitask learning approach also enabled NVM 1.0 to transfer knowledge effectively between domains, making it more efficient at solving problems that spanned multiple modalities.

Finally, Nvidia made extensive use of **resource-efficient scaling techniques**. By employing advanced parallel computing methods on their Megatron Core platform, they ensured that the training process was both faster and more efficient. This not only reduced the computational cost but also allowed for iterative improvements, ensuring that NVM 1.0 was continuously optimized throughout its development cycle.

The result of these innovations is a model that performs consistently and exceptionally across text-based and multimodal tasks. While competitors often struggle with performance degradation when integrating multiple domains, NVM 1.0 stands as a rare example of balance and precision. Nvidia's approach to training efficiency has not only solved a persistent problem in AI development but has also set a new standard for how future models can achieve excellence across modalities without compromise.

Chapter 4: Key Capabilities of NVM 1.0

Nvidia's NVM 1.0 redefines Optical Character Recognition (OCR) by moving beyond the basic ability to extract text from images. While traditional OCR systems are designed to recognize characters and words in static visual inputs, they often fail to understand the broader context of the text, especially in complex, real-world scenarios. NVM 1.0 addresses this limitation with remarkable precision, combining cutting-edge multimodal capabilities with contextual reasoning that elevates OCR to an entirely new level.

At its core, NVM 1.0's strength in OCR lies in its ability to process not just the text itself but the visual and structural elements of the image. This means it can interpret the layout of a document, identify relationships between different pieces of text, and derive meaning from the context in which the text appears. For example, when analyzing a scanned invoice, NVM 1.0 doesn't simply recognize individual words like "total" or "tax." It understands their significance within the structure of the document, allowing it to extract critical information such as totals, itemized details, and payment instructions with high accuracy.

This contextual understanding is made possible by NVM 1.0's **hybrid architecture** and **1D Tile Tagging** design. The model breaks down high-resolution images into smaller, manageable sections, or "tiles," and assigns tags that capture their content and spatial relationship within the image. This approach enables the model to focus on fine-grained details while maintaining an awareness of how each part fits into the whole. As a result, NVM 1.0 can process complex documents like forms, tables, and receipts with an unparalleled level of accuracy.

Beyond static text, NVM 1.0 excels at dynamic and handwritten inputs, a challenge where many OCR systems fall short. Whether it's analyzing a whiteboard filled with handwritten equations or extracting notes from a scanned paper document, the model not only recognizes the characters but also understands their context. For instance, in handwritten mathematical equations, NVM 1.0 can correctly identify variables, operators, and numerical values, then apply reasoning to solve the problem or provide step-by-step explanations.

One of the most groundbreaking aspects of NVM 1.0's OCR capabilities is its ability to summarize and interpret the extracted text. This goes far beyond merely converting images into editable text files. Imagine a legal document or a lengthy contract—NVM 1.0 doesn't just digitize the content; it can identify key sections, summarize critical points, and even answer questions about specific clauses. This ability to reason and provide actionable insights makes it invaluable in industries like law, finance, and healthcare, where efficiency and accuracy are paramount.

NVM 1.0's success in OCR extends to its performance on benchmarks, where it consistently delivers state-of-the-art results. On tasks like document analysis, it outperforms competitors by integrating vision and text-processing capabilities seamlessly. Unlike models that simply extract text and leave the interpretation to external systems, NVM 1.0 provides a comprehensive solution that combines recognition, reasoning, and contextual understanding.

In practical applications, this capability translates to significant advancements. Businesses can use NVM 1.0 to automate processes like invoice reconciliation, customer data extraction, or document summarization, reducing the need for manual intervention. Healthcare providers can digitize and interpret handwritten medical records, improving the speed and accuracy of patient care. Even creative industries, like publishing or advertising, can leverage NVM 1.0 to analyze visual content and generate targeted narratives based on the extracted text.

In essence, NVM 1.0 doesn't just excel at recognizing text in images—it reimagines what OCR can achieve by adding layers of contextual intelligence and reasoning. Its ability to process, interpret, and apply extracted information makes it a transformative tool, pushing the boundaries of what's possible in document analysis and visual data processing.

NVM 1.0 stands out in the AI landscape not just for its multimodal capabilities but for its exceptional reasoning power. Unlike many models that struggle when tasks demand advanced logic or problem-solving, NVM 1.0 excels at tackling intricate challenges in areas like math and coding. Its ability to interpret complex data, reason through problems, and deliver accurate solutions showcases why it is being hailed as a game changer in AI.

One of the most impressive aspects of NVM 1.0 is its proficiency in mathematical reasoning. While many models can identify numbers and symbols, few can truly understand and process equations in context, especially when presented in visual formats like handwritten notes or whiteboard sketches.

NVM 1.0 doesn't just stop at recognizing mathematical content—it goes further by solving equations and providing step-by-step explanations for its answers. Imagine a whiteboard filled with equations written during a classroom lecture or brainstorming session. NVM 1.0 can analyze the visual data, identify each equation, and calculate precise solutions, offering detailed reasoning for its process. This capability is a massive leap forward for educational tools, research applications, and even professional environments where interpreting complex mathematical data is a daily requirement.

In the realm of coding, NVM 1.0 demonstrates similar prowess. Coding often involves intricate logic and structured rules that can vary widely across languages and contexts. For example, developers may jot down handwritten pseudo-code on paper or a whiteboard during brainstorming sessions. Deciphering this pseudo-code, understanding its intent, and translating it into executable code has traditionally been beyond the scope of AI models. NVM 1.0 breaks this barrier by accurately interpreting handwritten pseudo-code, reasoning through its structure, and generating clean, functional code. Whether it's parsing conditional logic, loops, or function calls, the model not only deciphers the content but also ensures that the code aligns with the developer's intent.

Another standout feature is NVM 1.0's ability to summarize and explain its reasoning, which adds a layer of transparency and usability to its results. For instance, when solving a complex mathematical problem, the model doesn't just deliver the final answer; it walks through each step of the calculation, making its process easy to understand. Similarly, in coding tasks, NVM 1.0 can annotate its output, explaining the logic behind each line of code and offering suggestions for optimization. This capability transforms it from a mere tool into a collaborative partner for students, developers, and researchers.

A practical application of this reasoning power can be seen in fields like engineering and data science, where professionals often work with highly technical problems. For example, an engineer might use NVM 1.0 to analyze a visual diagram of equations and extract actionable insights. Similarly, a data scientist could rely on the model to debug a handwritten algorithm, ensuring accuracy and efficiency in their workflows. The potential extends to educational platforms as well, where NVM 1.0 can help students learn complex subjects interactively by breaking down problems and providing clear, step-by-step guidance.

What sets NVM 1.0 apart from its competitors is not just its ability to perform these tasks but its consistency and accuracy across various reasoning challenges. Many AI models experience performance degradation when asked to integrate visual and textual reasoning, but NVM 1.0 thrives in these scenarios. It combines its understanding of context, structure, and logic to deliver results that are not only accurate but also actionable and relevant to real-world applications.

In summary, NVM 1.0's reasoning power makes it an invaluable asset across multiple domains. Its ability to solve complex problems in math and coding, interpret handwritten inputs, and provide detailed explanations represents a significant leap forward in AI capabilities. This isn't just about making tasks easier—it's about enabling new possibilities in education, professional development, and technical problem-solving, firmly establishing NVM 1.0 as a model built for both innovation and impact.

NVM 1.0 is not just another AI model that processes input mechanically—it is designed to respond dynamically to user instructions, adapting its tone, depth, and style to suit diverse needs. This adaptability makes it one of the most versatile tools in AI, capable of catering to users ranging from professionals and educators to casual consumers. By tailoring its responses with remarkable precision, NVM 1.0 brings a level of personalization that feels intuitive and collaborative.

When responding to user input, NVM 1.0 demonstrates an ability to adjust its tone seamlessly. For instance, if a user requests a concise explanation, the model can distill complex concepts into a brief yet accurate summary. Conversely, when a user asks for a detailed breakdown, it expands its response with step-by-step reasoning, context, and examples. This flexibility is particularly useful in technical or educational settings, where different audiences often require varying levels of depth. A developer seeking debugging advice may want granular code-level details, while a student learning a new concept might prefer a simplified, high-level overview. NVM 1.0 excels at identifying and meeting these needs without compromising accuracy.

Beyond tone and depth, NVM 1.0 also adapts its responses to align with the user's intent. If the input is framed as a formal query—such as a business-related question or a research topic—the model adopts a professional, polished style. If the input is conversational or casual, the model matches the tone, making its responses feel approachable and relatable. This ability to mirror the user's communication style enhances the overall user experience, creating a sense of engagement that traditional AI models often lack.

One of the most exciting advancements in NVM 1.0's development is its ability to grasp humor and contextual subtleties, a leap forward in making AI feel more human-like. Humor, often regarded as one of the most complex facets of human communication, involves recognizing not only the literal meaning of words but also the underlying context, cultural references, and contrasts that make something amusing. NVM 1.0 showcases a remarkable capacity to interpret these layers, understanding not just what is being said but why it might be funny.

Consider, for example, a meme that juxtaposes a fierce lion labeled "Monday Motivation" with a sleepy kitten labeled "Actual Monday." NVM 1.0 doesn't merely recognize the text or identify the images; it understands the contrast and humor behind the labels. It can grasp that the lion symbolizes an aspirational, energetic mindset often associated with the beginning of the week, while the kitten represents the relatable reality of fatigue. This ability to interpret humor extends to jokes, puns, and even nuanced satire, making NVM 1.0 a valuable tool for content creation, entertainment, and social media analysis.

The model's contextual understanding plays a significant role in its ability to navigate humor. In addition to processing words and visuals, NVM 1.0 considers the broader scenario in which the content exists. For example, it can recognize when a sarcastic remark is made in response to an image or when a witty observation relies on the relationship between the text and its visual backdrop. This capability not only makes the model adept at humor but also enhances its ability to engage with users in a way that feels natural and intuitive.

The implications of these features are vast. NVM 1.0's ability to adapt its responses and grasp humor has practical applications in industries like customer engagement, marketing, and entertainment. Imagine an AI assistant that can provide information with just the right tone, whether it's a serious financial report or a lighthearted response to a casual inquiry. Similarly, in advertising or content creation, NVM 1.0 can analyze trends in humor and generate material that resonates with target audiences. In education, it can make learning more engaging by delivering information with wit and relatability, helping students connect with even the most challenging subjects.

In essence, NVM 1.0 bridges the gap between utility and personality. Its ability to tailor responses based on user input and understand humor represents a step toward AI that feels more intuitive, relatable, and human-like. These advancements not only make the model a versatile tool but also signal the beginning of a new era in human-AI interaction, where machines can truly adapt to the diverse needs and nuances of their users.

Chapter 5: Real-World Applications

In the healthcare industry, where precision and efficiency can mean the difference between life and death, NVM 1.0 stands out as a transformative tool. Its ability to digitize medical records, extract critical information, and provide actionable insights with exceptional accuracy positions it as a game changer in modern medicine. By addressing some of the most persistent challenges in healthcare, NVM 1.0 is not just a technological advancement—it's a potential lifesaver.

One of the key applications of NVM 1.0 in healthcare is its role in **digitizing medical records.** While many medical facilities have transitioned to electronic health records (EHRs), a significant amount of historical patient data still exists in handwritten or scanned formats. These documents, ranging from physician notes and lab reports to prescription records, are often difficult to process using conventional OCR systems. NVM 1.0 excels in this area by accurately extracting text from even the most complex or poorly written medical documents. Its advanced **1D Tile Tagging** mechanism allows it to handle high-resolution scans and handwritten notes with ease, ensuring that no critical detail is overlooked during digitization.

However, NVM 1.0 goes beyond basic text extraction. It also excels at **understanding context**, enabling it to interpret medical jargon, abbreviations, and complex relationships within patient records. For instance, it can differentiate between a diagnosis, a treatment plan, and a patient's medical history, organizing this information in a way that is both structured and meaningful. Imagine a doctor's handwritten note that includes a diagnosis of diabetes, a prescription for medication, and follow-up recommendations. NVM 1.0 can process this input, classify the relevant sections, and integrate them into a digital system that is easy for healthcare professionals to navigate.

The model's **reasoning capabilities** further enhance its impact in healthcare. By analyzing digitized records in conjunction with new patient data, NVM 1.0 can identify patterns or anomalies that may not be immediately apparent to human practitioners. For example, it can flag potential drug interactions based on a patient's medication history or suggest additional tests based on patterns in their lab results. This level of insight empowers healthcare providers to make more informed decisions, improving patient outcomes while reducing the risk of errors.

Another critical application of NVM 1.0 is its ability to **process and summarize large volumes of medical data.** Healthcare professionals are often inundated with information, from test results and imaging scans to clinical trial data and research papers. NVM 1.0 can parse through these documents quickly and extract key insights, presenting them in a concise and actionable format. For example, it could analyze a complex patient case, summarize relevant findings, and highlight the most critical factors that require attention—all within moments. This allows doctors to focus more on patient care and less on administrative burdens.

The implications for healthcare are profound, particularly in scenarios where time is of the essence. In emergency situations, such as treating trauma patients or managing outbreaks, NVM 1.0's ability to rapidly process and analyze medical records can save precious time. By delivering accurate, context-aware insights instantly, it helps healthcare providers make swift, informed decisions that can save lives.

Beyond individual patient care, NVM 1.0 also has the potential to impact **public health initiatives.** Its ability to analyze large datasets, such as anonymized patient records or epidemiological data, can help identify trends, predict outbreaks, and inform policy decisions. For example, during a disease outbreak, the model could analyze patient symptoms, travel histories, and treatment outcomes to identify patterns and help allocate resources more effectively.

Accuracy is paramount in healthcare, and NVM 1.0 delivers it consistently. By eliminating the errors that often arise in manual data processing and enhancing the precision of insights, it reduces risks and enhances trust in AI-driven medical solutions. Whether it's helping doctors provide better care, streamlining administrative tasks, or contributing to public health efforts, NVM 1.0 is poised to revolutionize the way healthcare systems operate.

In a field where every second and every detail matter, NVM 1.0's ability to digitize, interpret, and apply medical information with precision is not just innovative—it's lifesaving. This model represents a new era in healthcare, where cutting-edge AI works alongside professionals to deliver faster, smarter, and more effective care to patients worldwide.

In the fast-paced world of finance, where accuracy and efficiency are paramount, NVM 1.0 emerges as a powerful tool for automating tedious processes like invoice and receipt management. Businesses and financial institutions, often dealing with massive volumes of transactional data, require tools that can not only process this information but also extract actionable insights with minimal errors. NVM 1.0's multimodal capabilities make it uniquely suited for this task.

One of its key strengths is its ability to process **scanned invoices and receipts** with extraordinary precision. Traditional systems often struggle with the variability in formats, layouts, and text quality found in financial documents. From handwritten expense receipts to digitally generated invoices with complex tables, NVM 1.0 can analyze these inputs with ease. Thanks to its **1D Tile Tagging** mechanism, the model can focus on small but crucial details within high-resolution scans, ensuring every number, line item, and label is accurately captured.

Beyond merely extracting text, NVM 1.0 excels in **contextual understanding.** It can distinguish between headers like "Invoice Number" or "Due Date" and the corresponding values, seamlessly categorizing and organizing the data. For instance, in a multi-page invoice, NVM 1.0 can identify subtotal calculations, taxes, and the final amount while flagging discrepancies if the math doesn't add up. This kind of contextual insight minimizes the need for human intervention, saving significant time and reducing costly errors.

The model's **reasoning abilities** also play a critical role in streamlining finance operations. For example, NVM 1.0 can cross-reference information from multiple receipts or invoices to detect duplicate claims, identify inconsistencies, or even flag unusual patterns that may indicate fraud. In accounts payable workflows, the model can automate approval processes by verifying details against pre-defined criteria, such as vendor information or payment terms, ensuring compliance and speeding up operations.

For businesses, this level of automation translates into considerable cost savings. Manual data entry, reconciliation, and validation—tasks that traditionally required hours of work—can now be completed in minutes with higher accuracy. Financial teams can reallocate their resources toward more strategic activities, such as financial analysis and decision-making, rather than being bogged down by administrative tasks.

NVM 1.0's capabilities also benefit small businesses and freelancers, who often lack the resources for dedicated financial teams. By digitizing and organizing their financial records effortlessly, the model enables them to stay on top of cash flow, tax documentation, and expense tracking, empowering better financial management.

In the realm of education, NVM 1.0 shines as a versatile tool that makes learning more accessible, engaging, and personalized. Its exceptional ability to handle math, coding, and reasoning tasks positions it as an ideal companion for students, educators, and institutions alike. The model's adaptability ensures that it can cater to learners at all levels, from elementary students to advanced researchers.

One of its standout features is its ability to provide **step-by-step explanations** for complex subjects, especially in mathematics. Traditional educational tools often focus solely on providing answers, leaving students with little understanding of how to arrive at the solution. NVM 1.0 takes a different approach by breaking problems down into manageable steps, offering detailed reasoning at every stage. For instance, when presented with a complex algebraic equation, the model doesn't just supply the answer—it explains each calculation, why specific steps are taken, and how the solution is derived. This interactive approach fosters deeper understanding and builds problem-solving skills.

In coding, NVM 1.0 proves to be an invaluable resource for both beginners and advanced learners. For novice coders, the model can interpret handwritten pseudo-code or partially completed programs and transform them into executable code while providing detailed commentary on how the code works. For more advanced learners, it can debug errors, optimize existing code, and even suggest alternative approaches for efficiency and scalability. By bridging the gap between abstract concepts and practical implementation, NVM 1.0 enables students to build confidence and competence in programming.

Beyond individual subjects, NVM 1.0's **adaptability to instruction** enhances its role as an educational tool. It tailors its responses to the user's needs, providing concise explanations for quick clarification or expanding on topics for in-depth understanding. Imagine a student preparing for an exam who needs quick summaries of key topics one day and detailed walkthroughs of challenging problems the next—NVM 1.0 can seamlessly adjust to both scenarios.

The model's ability to **analyze and interpret visual data** further expands its potential in education. For example, it can explain concepts using diagrams, analyze graphs in science or economics, and even assist in understanding annotated charts in history or geography. This multimodal capability makes learning more dynamic and interactive, breaking down the barriers between textual and visual comprehension.

NVM 1.0's impact in education extends to educators themselves, who can use it to create tailored lesson plans, generate practice questions, or even design interactive quizzes. Its ability to process diverse datasets and reason across modalities ensures that teaching materials are accurate, engaging, and customized to the needs of the students.

Ultimately, NVM 1.0 is transforming education by making learning more interactive, personalized, and effective. Whether it's helping a student grasp the fundamentals of algebra, guiding a budding coder through their first project, or enabling educators to craft better learning experiences, this AI model is paving the way for a smarter and more connected educational landscape.

NVM 1.0 brings a new level of innovation to content creation, offering capabilities that make it an indispensable tool in industries such as advertising, storytelling, and entertainment. Its ability to analyze and generate creative content with contextually rich insights sets it apart from other AI models, allowing creators to unlock new levels of efficiency and imagination.

One of its standout features is its **capacity to analyze creative trends and tailor content to meet specific goals.** In advertising, for instance, NVM 1.0 can process large datasets of consumer behavior, market trends, and previous campaign successes to identify patterns that resonate with target audiences. It doesn't just stop at data analysis—it uses this information to generate creative copy, slogans, or taglines that align perfectly with a brand's messaging. For example, an advertising agency can input details about a product, its target demographic, and desired tone, and NVM 1.0 will generate a campaign that speaks directly to that audience, offering both inspiration and actionable ideas.

In storytelling, NVM 1.0's ability to understand context and narrative structure makes it a powerful partner for writers and creators. It can analyze existing stories, identifying themes, character arcs, and tonal elements, and use this understanding to generate original narratives that feel fresh and engaging. For example, an author struggling with writer's block could input a rough outline or a list of character traits, and NVM 1.0 would expand on these ideas, suggesting plot twists, dialogue, or even full scenes that align with the intended tone and pacing. Whether crafting a screenplay, developing a video game storyline, or creating content for episodic media, the model's contextual awareness ensures that its outputs are coherent, imaginative, and adaptable to the creator's vision.

Entertainment platforms, particularly those producing content for social media or digital campaigns, benefit immensely from NVM 1.0's ability to integrate **visual and textual inputs**. It can analyze images or videos, interpret their themes and emotional tones, and generate complementary captions or descriptions. For instance, a filmmaker could upload a series of mood-board images for a project, and NVM 1.0 could draft synopses, promotional materials, or even dialogue that aligns with the visual style and atmosphere. This ability to seamlessly combine text and visuals makes it an invaluable tool for multimedia storytelling.

NVM 1.0 also excels in **creative problem-solving.** When presented with vague or incomplete ideas, it bridges the gaps with suggestions that are both innovative and practical. Imagine a marketing team brainstorming for a holiday campaign—they could input a theme like "nostalgia" or "family togetherness," and NVM 1.0 would provide creative concepts, from ad copy to social media strategies, all designed to evoke the desired emotional response.

Another transformative aspect of NVM 1.0 is its ability to tailor content to diverse audiences and cultural contexts. By analyzing regional preferences, linguistic nuances, and cultural trends, the model ensures that its outputs are not only creative but also relevant and resonant. This is especially valuable in global campaigns, where a single piece of content may need to be adapted for multiple markets without losing its core message.

In the realm of entertainment, NVM 1.0 has the potential to revolutionize how audiences engage with content. It can be used to create interactive experiences, such as choose-your-own-adventure narratives or personalized content recommendations based on user preferences. Its understanding of humor, tone, and emotion allows it to generate content that feels deeply human, whether it's crafting witty one-liners for a comedy sketch or poignant dialogue for a drama.

For independent creators, NVM 1.0 is a powerful ally, offering tools that amplify creativity without requiring extensive resources. It can generate ideas, refine drafts, or provide stylistic enhancements, empowering individuals to produce professional-quality content at scale. For large teams, it acts as an accelerant, cutting down on the time needed for ideation and execution while ensuring outputs remain fresh and impactful.

Ultimately, NVM 1.0's ability to analyze, adapt, and generate creative content positions it as a cornerstone for the future of content creation. It is not just a tool for efficiency—it is a collaborator that inspires, streamlines, and elevates the creative process, making it an invaluable resource for industries that thrive on imagination and innovation. Whether in advertising, storytelling, or entertainment, NVM 1.0 proves that AI can not only support creativity but actively drive it forward.

NVM 1.0 has emerged as a transformative tool in the fields of engineering and data science, offering unparalleled capabilities to solve technical problems with speed and precision. In disciplines where complex calculations, data analysis, and troubleshooting are integral, NVM 1.0's multimodal abilities and reasoning power provide a competitive edge, enabling professionals to work more efficiently and accurately than ever before.

One of the model's most impactful features in engineering is its ability to process **visual data alongside technical information.** For instance, in mechanical or structural engineering, professionals often rely on detailed diagrams, blueprints, or CAD drawings to design and analyze systems. NVM 1.0 can interpret these visual inputs, identify critical components, and extract meaningful insights. For example, an engineer could upload a schematic of a machine or a structural diagram of a building, and the model would identify potential weak points, suggest optimizations, or even flag design inconsistencies. This ability to integrate visual analysis with textual reasoning allows engineers to troubleshoot and improve designs faster than traditional methods.

In the field of **data science**, NVM 1.0 excels at handling large and complex datasets, a task that often requires both mathematical precision and contextual understanding. Data scientists frequently deal with diverse formats of information, from structured tables to unstructured logs and graphs. NVM 1.0's multimodal architecture allows it to process these inputs seamlessly, offering advanced analytics and insights. For example, it can analyze trends in a dataset, detect anomalies, and provide statistical summaries, all while presenting its findings in a clear, actionable format. This makes it an invaluable resource for everything from exploratory data analysis to predictive modeling.

When tackling coding-related challenges, NVM 1.0 shines as a **technical assistant** capable of interpreting pseudo-code, debugging errors, and optimizing codebases. Engineers and data scientists often need to write algorithms to analyze or process data, but debugging or enhancing these algorithms can be time-consuming. NVM 1.0 can analyze handwritten or digitally input pseudo-code, identify logical errors, and provide optimized, executable versions. For example, a data scientist working on a machine learning pipeline might input a partially written script, and NVM 1.0 could complete it, explain the functionality, and suggest refinements to improve efficiency or scalability.

The model's reasoning power extends to **mathematical problem-solving**, a critical skill in both engineering and data science. Whether solving equations related to structural stress, heat transfer, or fluid dynamics, NVM 1.0 excels at delivering step-by-step solutions that are both accurate and easy to understand. Data scientists, on the other hand, can rely on the model for advanced statistical analysis, including regression modeling, hypothesis testing, and optimization algorithms. Its ability to reason through complex problems and provide clear explanations makes it a valuable teaching tool as well, helping professionals and students alike deepen their understanding of technical concepts.

Another area where NVM 1.0 proves invaluable is in **collaborative problem-solving**. Engineering and data science often involve teams working across disciplines, where clear communication of ideas is critical. NVM 1.0 can serve as a bridge, synthesizing complex technical jargon into accessible summaries that can be understood by non-technical stakeholders. For example, it could generate a summary of a detailed engineering report for project managers or translate a complex data visualization into actionable business insights for decision-makers. This capability ensures that all team members are aligned, regardless of their technical expertise.

The model's utility doesn't stop at analysis—it also accelerates innovation by **proposing creative solutions to technical challenges.** In engineering, this might mean suggesting alternative materials or designs to improve efficiency or reduce costs. In data science, it could involve identifying overlooked data relationships or proposing novel algorithms to enhance predictive accuracy. Its ability to reason contextually ensures that its suggestions are not only innovative but also practical and implementable.

The speed and accuracy with which NVM 1.0 operates offer tangible benefits across industries that depend on engineering and data science. In aerospace, it can optimize flight simulations or analyze the structural integrity of components. In manufacturing, it can improve production processes by analyzing sensor data and predicting equipment failures before they occur. In data-intensive fields like finance or healthcare, it can process massive datasets in real time, uncovering trends and insights that drive better decision-making.

Ultimately, NVM 1.0 represents a new standard in technical problem-solving. Its ability to handle complex calculations, analyze visual data, and deliver clear, actionable solutions makes it an indispensable tool for engineers and data scientists. By automating routine tasks and accelerating the resolution of complex challenges, it not only boosts productivity but also frees up professionals to focus on innovation and strategic decision-making, ensuring that they remain at the forefront of their respective fields.

Chapter 6: Setting New Standards in the AI Industry

Nvidia's decision to release the model weights and training code for NVM 1.0 via its Megatron Core platform represents a bold and forward-thinking step toward democratizing AI innovation. By making this cutting-edge technology openly accessible, Nvidia is breaking down barriers that have traditionally limited access to state-of-the-art AI tools, enabling researchers, developers, and organizations worldwide to build upon its advancements.

In the AI community, access to advanced models and training resources is often restricted due to proprietary systems or high computational costs. This exclusivity has historically limited innovation to a select few well-funded institutions or tech giants, creating a disparity in who can meaningfully contribute to the field. Nvidia's open-source approach with NVM 1.0 disrupts this status quo, leveling the playing field and empowering a broader range of participants to engage with, modify, and deploy the model for their unique needs.

By releasing the model weights, Nvidia is providing researchers and developers with the foundation they need to explore new applications without having to start from scratch. These weights encapsulate the intelligence NVM 1.0 has gained through extensive training on diverse datasets, saving users the time and computational resources required to train a large-scale model themselves. Whether it's a university lab experimenting with niche AI applications or a small startup aiming to innovate in a specific industry, access to these pre-trained weights offers a significant head start.

The availability of the training code via Megatron Core further enhances accessibility, offering developers the tools and frameworks needed to fine-tune or extend NVM 1.0 for specialized use cases. For example, a healthcare-focused AI team could adapt the model to process specific types of medical data, or a financial technology company could customize it for analyzing market trends and forecasts. This ability to tailor the model to diverse industries and applications fosters innovation that might not have been possible under a closed-source framework.

Open-sourcing NVM 1.0 also encourages **collaboration and collective progress.** Researchers can share findings, propose improvements, and work together to address limitations, accelerating the model's evolution and applicability. This communal effort benefits not only the AI community but also the industries and end-users who rely on AI-driven solutions. By enabling the global talent pool to contribute to its development, Nvidia ensures that NVM 1.0's potential will continue to grow, reaching far beyond its initial release.

Nvidia's decision is particularly noteworthy in light of the broader AI landscape, where competition among tech giants often leads to proprietary advancements that remain behind closed doors. By contrast, Nvidia is embracing an open-source ethos, signaling a shift toward more inclusive innovation. This move challenges other industry leaders to reconsider their approaches and potentially adopt similar practices, fostering a culture of transparency and shared progress across the AI field.

The decision to release NVM 1.0 as open source also has practical implications for smaller organizations and independent developers. With limited budgets, these entities often face steep challenges in adopting AI technology due to the high costs of infrastructure and proprietary tools. Access to NVM 1.0's weights and training code eliminates many of these barriers, empowering smaller players to compete on a more level playing field with larger corporations. This democratization of technology enables a wave of innovation that could produce breakthroughs in areas ranging from education to public health to environmental sustainability.

Finally, the decision reflects Nvidia's broader commitment to advancing the state of AI not as a competitive tool but as a shared resource for solving real-world problems. By removing obstacles to access, the company is fostering an environment where AI can be used to address challenges on a global scale, from improving disaster response systems to enhancing resource allocation in underserved communities.

In essence, Nvidia's open-source release of NVM 1.0 is more than just a technological milestone—it is a statement about the future of AI. By prioritizing accessibility and collaboration, Nvidia is empowering a new generation of innovators to harness the power of AI, ensuring that its benefits are distributed widely and equitably. This decision doesn't just make cutting-edge AI available; it sets the stage for a future where technology is a shared tool for collective progress.

The release of NVM 1.0 has sent shockwaves through the AI community, forcing industry leaders like OpenAI, Meta, and Google to take notice. Nvidia's model has disrupted the competitive landscape by addressing long-standing limitations in multimodal AI while setting new benchmarks for performance and accessibility. It's not just a technological milestone—it's a clear challenge to the status quo that compels these competitors to rethink their strategies.

For years, OpenAI, Meta, and Google have dominated the AI field with their flagship models—GPT-4, Intern VL2, and advancements in Google's AI research, respectively. Each of these companies has made significant strides in either text-based or multimodal tasks, but often with trade-offs. OpenAI's GPT-4 is a leader in natural language processing, yet it lags in seamlessly integrating vision and language tasks. Meta's Intern VL2 focuses heavily on multimodal performance but often sacrifices text accuracy, and Google's AI models, while versatile, remain largely proprietary, limiting their impact on broader innovation.

Nvidia's NVM 1.0, by contrast, offers a cohesive solution that excels in both text-based reasoning and multimodal tasks, effectively erasing the compromises that other models have struggled with. Its ability to handle tasks across domains with equal precision—not just performing well, but often surpassing its competitors—sets a new standard for what an AI model can achieve. Whether it's optical character recognition, visual question answering, coding, or mathematical reasoning, NVM 1.0 demonstrates consistency and excellence that forces other players to respond.

The open-source release of NVM 1.0 further intensifies its impact. While companies like OpenAI and Meta have traditionally guarded their most advanced models, Nvidia's decision to share the model weights and training code via Megatron Core democratizes access to state-of-the-art AI. This move not only accelerates innovation across industries but also pressures competitors to consider more inclusive approaches to their own technology. The question is no longer just about who can build the best model but who can empower the global AI community to benefit from it.

Competitors now face a dilemma: stick to closed-source practices and risk falling behind in adoption and influence, or embrace a more open approach to remain relevant. Nvidia's strategic decision has fundamentally shifted the dynamics of AI development, prompting discussions about collaboration, transparency, and the democratization of technology at a global scale.

One of the most significant breakthroughs of NVM 1.0 is its ability to solve the long-standing trade-off between excelling in multimodal tasks and maintaining top-tier text-based accuracy. For years, AI developers have grappled with the challenge of creating models that can integrate text and vision capabilities without compromising their strengths in either domain. NVM 1.0 shatters this barrier, proving that it's possible to achieve exceptional performance in both areas simultaneously.

Traditional multimodal models have often prioritized one modality over the other. Models like Intern VL2 excel at vision-language tasks but suffer from noticeable degradation in text-based benchmarks, such as coding or logical reasoning. Even models like Llama 3v attempt to preserve text accuracy by freezing certain components during multimodal training, but this approach limits their ability to improve across both domains. This compromise has long been seen as an unavoidable consequence of integrating multiple modalities.

NVM 1.0's hybrid architecture changes the game entirely. By combining decoder-only frameworks optimized for text tasks with cross-attention mechanisms designed for multimodal reasoning, the model achieves a harmonious balance that allows it to perform exceptionally well across diverse benchmarks. Unlike its competitors, NVM 1.0 doesn't sacrifice text accuracy to improve multimodal capabilities—it enhances both.

The impact of this breakthrough is most evident in its benchmark results. For example, NVM 1.0's performance on OCR tasks and visual question answering (VQA) is state-of-the-art, while its accuracy in text-based domains like coding and math reasoning has improved by a remarkable 4.3 points. This dual strength enables NVM 1.0 to handle tasks that require seamless transitions between text and visuals, such as analyzing documents, solving equations, or interpreting diagrams with explanatory text. The result is a model that feels equally at home processing technical reports as it does analyzing complex images.

This ability to bridge modalities without compromise is not just a technical achievement—it's a fundamental shift in how AI is developed and applied. For industries that rely on AI for real-world problem-solving, the elimination of these trade-offs means more reliable, versatile tools that can tackle a broader range of challenges.

Whether in healthcare, finance, or education, NVM 1.0's balanced capabilities translate to faster workflows, fewer errors, and greater overall impact.

By erasing the need to choose between multimodal excellence and text-based accuracy, Nvidia has redefined the expectations for what AI can achieve. NVM 1.0 doesn't just raise the bar—it establishes a new standard for performance, one that competitors will now have to meet or exceed. In doing so, Nvidia has cemented its position as a leader in AI innovation, setting the stage for the next generation of intelligent systems that truly excel in every domain.

NVM 1.0 represents more than just a milestone in artificial intelligence—it serves as a blueprint for the future of AI. Nvidia's latest model is a clear indicator of where the industry is headed, showing how advanced architecture, versatility, and open access can converge to redefine what's possible. By solving long-standing challenges and pushing the boundaries of multimodal and text-based AI, NVM

1.0 sets the stage for the next generation of intelligent systems.

At the heart of this blueprint is **seamless multimodal integration.** For years, AI models have excelled within specific domains, but the future demands systems capable of synthesizing information from diverse data types. NVM 1.0 proves that it's possible to bridge the gap between vision and text without compromise, paving the way for AI models that can operate across modalities with precision and fluidity. This isn't just about excelling at benchmarks—it's about creating AI that understands and interacts with the world in a human-like way, where information isn't siloed but integrated into a cohesive understanding.

Another defining feature of NVM 1.0's vision for the future is its **dual strength** across tasks. As industries evolve, the demand for AI that can handle a variety of complex challenges will only grow. Models like NVM 1.0, which excel at both text-heavy reasoning and visual problem-solving, demonstrate that the future of AI lies in versatility. Whether it's solving equations, interpreting technical diagrams, or generating creative content, next-generation AI must be capable of adapting to a diverse range of applications while maintaining top-tier performance.

Nvidia's **open-source strategy** with NVM 1.0 also points to a future where AI innovation becomes more collaborative and inclusive. By releasing the model weights and training code via Megatron Core, Nvidia has made cutting-edge technology accessible to a broader audience. This decision doesn't just democratize AI—it sets a precedent for how future models can inspire global innovation. Researchers, developers, and startups now have the tools to experiment, adapt, and build on NVM 1.0, ensuring that its impact extends far beyond Nvidia's labs. This collaborative ethos will likely shape the next generation of AI, fostering a community-driven approach to solving global challenges.

The emphasis on **quality over quantity** in training data is another critical aspect of NVM 1.0's legacy. As AI systems become more advanced, the need for clean, diverse, and contextually relevant data will grow. NVM 1.0's success in improving both multimodal and text-based capabilities demonstrates that training with carefully curated datasets yields better results than relying on sheer volume alone. Future models will likely adopt similar strategies, focusing on data diversity and contextual richness to achieve more reliable and precise performance.

NVM 1.0 also highlights the importance of **real-world applicability** in AI design. Its ability to handle practical challenges, from digitizing medical records to processing financial documents, underscores a broader trend: the next wave of AI won't just be research-focused; it will be built for deployment in everyday scenarios. The model's performance isn't limited to theoretical benchmarks—it's tailored to meet the needs of industries like healthcare, finance, education, and entertainment. This shift toward practical, production-grade AI is a cornerstone of the future, where technology seamlessly integrates into workflows and enhances decision-making across sectors.

Looking ahead, NVM 1.0's hybrid architecture offers a roadmap for improving future AI models. By combining the strengths of decoder-only and cross-attention-based systems, Nvidia has shown how architectural innovation can resolve long-standing trade-offs. Future models will likely expand on this principle, creating even more efficient and flexible systems capable of handling increasingly complex tasks.

Finally, NVM 1.0's success reinforces the importance of **user-centered AI.** Its ability to adapt responses based on user input, tailor outputs to specific needs, and even grasp complex humor signals a shift toward more intuitive, human-like interaction. As AI continues to evolve, the focus will increasingly be on creating systems that don't just perform tasks but engage with users in meaningful, personalized ways. The future of AI isn't just about intelligence—it's about accessibility, relatability, and collaboration.

In many ways, NVM 1.0 isn't just a model—it's a vision for what AI can become. By addressing today's challenges and setting new standards for performance, versatility, and openness, it lays the foundation for a new era of artificial intelligence. The next generation of AI models will build on this blueprint, advancing in ways that make technology more powerful, more accessible, and more transformative for society as a whole.

Chapter 7: Challenges and Implications

Making cutting-edge AI models freely available presents a fascinating and complex dilemma, one that is both a beacon of possibility and a source of potential concern. The decision to open-source advanced technology like Nvidia's NVM 1.0 is a bold move that holds the promise of democratizing innovation while simultaneously inviting challenges that could shape the trajectory of AI's future.

The benefits of open access are undeniable. By releasing the model weights and training code to the public, Nvidia is effectively tearing down the barriers that have historically limited AI development to a small circle of well-funded tech giants and academic institutions. This act of democratization enables researchers, startups, and independent developers from all corners of the world to engage with state-of-the-art tools. For those without the financial or computational resources to train such a model from scratch, having access to pre-trained weights is like being handed the keys to a high-performance vehicle. It opens the door to countless opportunities for experimentation, innovation, and the creation of specialized applications that might never have been imagined otherwise.

This spirit of collaboration has the potential to accelerate breakthroughs across industries. Healthcare teams can adapt the model to analyze patient data more effectively, educational platforms can tailor it to create personalized learning tools, and small businesses can use it to automate workflows that were previously out of reach. The open-source nature of NVM 1.0 amplifies its impact by inviting a global community of thinkers to refine, enhance, and expand its capabilities. It is no longer a solitary leap forward by a single company; it becomes a collective stride into the future of AI.

Yet, with this openness comes significant risks that cannot be overlooked. The accessibility of advanced AI also lowers the barriers for misuse. Bad actors could repurpose the model for malicious ends, whether it's generating convincing disinformation, creating deepfakes, or automating cyberattacks. With such a powerful tool in the hands of anyone with the expertise to deploy it, the line between innovation and exploitation becomes perilously thin. The same capabilities that can revolutionize industries can also undermine societal trust, security, and privacy if wielded irresponsibly.

Ethical concerns also loom large. When AI is made freely available, it becomes increasingly difficult to monitor how it is used. Models like NVM 1.0, capable of processing sensitive data or making decisions based on contextual information, could inadvertently perpetuate biases or discriminatory practices if applied carelessly. For example, using the model in hiring processes or financial risk assessments without appropriate safeguards could lead to unintended consequences, harming individuals and reinforcing systemic inequalities.

There's also the question of economic impact. While democratizing access is a noble goal, it might disrupt industries where proprietary AI development has been a key differentiator. Open-source models could level the playing field, but they could also destabilize established markets and force organizations to rethink their strategies to remain competitive. Smaller players may still struggle to keep up, as open access doesn't eliminate the need for technical expertise or infrastructure to deploy these tools effectively.

The open-source approach also introduces security vulnerabilities. With the code and model weights freely available, there's a risk of reverse engineering or manipulation. Malicious actors could modify the model to perform tasks beyond its intended design, potentially creating unforeseen dangers. These risks extend beyond digital spaces, with implications for critical infrastructure, national security, and even global stability.

Navigating this dilemma requires a delicate balance. The potential of open-source AI to drive progress must be weighed against the need for safeguards to prevent misuse. Licensing agreements that restrict unethical applications, robust security measures to protect against manipulation, and a commitment to transparency in how the model is used are all essential. Collaboration between AI developers, governments, and ethical organizations can help establish guidelines to ensure that the benefits of open access outweigh the risks.

Ultimately, the open-source dilemma encapsulates the dual nature of technology: its capacity to empower and to endanger. Nvidia's decision to release NVM 1.0 is both a testament to their confidence in the model's potential and a call to the global AI community to rise to the challenge of using it responsibly. It is a step toward a future where innovation is shared and transformative, but also one that requires vigilance to ensure this shared power is wielded wisely. The story of open-source AI is one of possibilities and responsibilities intertwined—a reflection of the immense complexity and promise of the technology itself.

The release of NVM 1.0 as an open-source model has set the stage for a new era of competition in the AI industry. Nvidia's bold move to democratize access to cutting-edge technology has not only elevated the capabilities of AI but also disrupted the strategies of its major rivals. Industry giants like OpenAI, Meta, and Google now find themselves at a crossroads, facing the pressure to respond to a model that challenges the traditional, closed-source development practices that have defined much of their work.

Historically, companies like OpenAI and Google have built their reputations on proprietary models that dominate specific domains. OpenAI's GPT-4, for instance, is a leader in natural language processing, while Google's AI initiatives excel in areas like search and recommendation systems. Meta, on the other hand, has focused heavily on multimodal AI, positioning its Intern VL2 as a strong competitor in vision-language integration. Each of these organizations has followed a strategy of controlled access, prioritizing the protection of intellectual property and market dominance. Nvidia's decision to release NVM 1.0 as open source fundamentally challenges this model, forcing competitors to reconsider whether their closed ecosystems are sustainable in a rapidly evolving landscape.

The immediate pressure stems from the fact that open-source models like NVM 1.0 are no longer just academic tools—they're production-grade systems capable of solving real-world problems. By making its model weights and training code freely available, Nvidia has handed researchers, startups, and even smaller companies a tool that rivals or surpasses the proprietary offerings of these tech giants. This democratization of AI development not only levels the playing field but also threatens to erode the competitive advantages that proprietary models once enjoyed.

Competitors now face a difficult question: Should they hold their ground with proprietary models or embrace open-source practices themselves? The answer is far from straightforward. For companies like OpenAI, which rely on subscription-based access to their models, embracing open source could undermine their revenue streams. Similarly, Google's AI initiatives often serve as the backbone of their broader ecosystem, from search to advertising. Opening these systems could jeopardize their market position and expose valuable intellectual property.

However, resisting the open-source trend comes with its own risks. Nvidia's decision has already sparked excitement and engagement across the global AI community, fostering collaboration and innovation at an unprecedented pace. If OpenAI, Meta, and Google fail to adapt, they risk being perceived as gatekeepers in a field that increasingly values transparency and accessibility. Moreover, as the community builds upon open-source models like NVM 1.0, competitors may find themselves outpaced not only in innovation but also in public trust and adoption.

Some rivals may take a hybrid approach, combining the strengths of proprietary systems with selective open-source initiatives. This strategy would allow them to retain control over core technologies while fostering collaboration on less sensitive aspects. For example, a company like Google might open-source specific components of its AI architecture, such as pre-trained weights for specific tasks, while keeping the broader model proprietary. Such a move could signal a willingness to participate in the collaborative AI ecosystem without fully relinquishing their competitive edge.

Meta, which has already embraced partial open-sourcing with its Llama series, might feel emboldened to go further. By making advanced models more accessible, they could position themselves as leaders in ethical and community-driven AI, capitalizing on the goodwill that often accompanies open-source efforts. However, they will also need to balance this with the need to maintain commercial viability and ensure that their innovations aren't misused.

The impact of Nvidia's decision goes beyond individual companies; it sets a precedent that could reshape the entire industry. As the competition heats up, companies will need to decide whether to cling to exclusivity or embrace the collaborative spirit of open source. Those that adapt quickly may find themselves leading the next wave of AI innovation, while those that resist could risk losing relevance in an ecosystem that increasingly values accessibility and shared progress.

Ultimately, Nvidia's release of NVM 1.0 has done more than just introduce a powerful AI model—it has redefined the rules of the game. The question now is not just who can build the best AI but who can do so in a way that empowers the world while staying competitive. In this new landscape, the companies that rise to the challenge will be the ones that strike the delicate balance between innovation, openness, and responsibility. The industry's next moves will be watched closely, as they will likely determine not only the future of AI competition but also the very nature of how artificial intelligence evolves in the years to come.

The advent of advanced multimodal AI models like NVM 1.0 brings immense potential to transform industries, but it also introduces a range of ethical considerations that cannot be ignored. As AI becomes more powerful and accessible, its ability to process and generate both text and visual data raises serious concerns about misuse, particularly in sensitive sectors such as healthcare, finance, and media. These challenges are not just hypothetical—they highlight the critical need for safeguards and accountability to ensure AI serves as a force for good.

One of the most pressing ethical concerns is the potential for **misuse in creating and spreading disinformation.** With its ability to analyze and generate both textual and visual content, a model like NVM 1.0 could be weaponized to create hyper-realistic fake news articles, fabricated images, or even deepfake videos that are indistinguishable from authentic media. Such tools could easily be exploited to manipulate public opinion, disrupt political processes, or fuel social unrest. While open access fosters innovation, it also lowers the barrier for bad actors to misuse this technology, amplifying the impact of false narratives on a global scale.

Another area of concern is **privacy and surveillance.** NVM 1.0's ability to process high-resolution images and extract contextual information from documents makes it a powerful tool for tasks like document digitization and analysis. However, in the wrong hands, these capabilities could be repurposed for invasive surveillance or data harvesting. For instance, organizations or governments could misuse the technology to extract personal information from scanned documents or monitor individuals without their consent. The potential for mass data collection, paired with the model's ability to analyze and interpret such data, raises serious questions about how privacy can be protected in an era of increasingly powerful AI.

In sensitive industries like **healthcare**, where accuracy and trust are paramount, the misuse of AI could have life-altering consequences. While NVM 1.0 can digitize medical records, extract critical information, and assist in diagnostics, its application must be carefully monitored. Misuse in this domain could include biased decision-making based on incomplete or skewed datasets, leading to inequities in treatment or misdiagnoses. The stakes are particularly high when patient outcomes depend on the reliability of AI-driven recommendations.

Similarly, in **finance**, where NVM 1.0's ability to process invoices, receipts, and transactional data offers immense efficiency, misuse could lead to catastrophic consequences. For example, malicious actors could exploit the model to analyze stolen financial documents, automate fraudulent activities, or identify vulnerabilities in financial systems. Such risks underscore the importance of developing robust safeguards to prevent unauthorized or unethical use of AI in critical economic infrastructures.

The potential for **bias and discrimination** is another significant challenge. Like all AI models, NVM 1.0 is only as unbiased as the data on which it is trained. If the training datasets reflect societal biases—whether in language, imagery, or decision-making processes—the model could inadvertently perpetuate those biases. In scenarios like hiring, loan approvals, or law enforcement, the misuse of AI could lead to discriminatory outcomes, disproportionately affecting marginalized communities. Addressing bias requires a commitment to transparency, continuous evaluation, and the incorporation of diverse, high-quality datasets that reflect the complexities of the real world.

Beyond individual industries, the ethical implications of **autonomy and decision-making** also come into play. As AI becomes more capable of interpreting context and making decisions, questions arise about the appropriate boundaries of its autonomy. For example, how much decision-making authority should an AI have in critical areas like healthcare diagnostics or financial approvals? At what point does reliance on AI undermine human accountability? These questions highlight the need for clear guidelines to define the roles and limitations of AI in decision-making processes.

To address these ethical challenges, a multifaceted approach is essential. First, developers must integrate **safeguards and monitoring mechanisms** into AI models to prevent misuse. This could include implementing usage restrictions, such as licensing agreements that prohibit unethical applications like surveillance or disinformation campaigns. Second, transparency is key—both in how the models are developed and how they are applied. Organizations using AI must be held accountable for their deployment practices and ensure that users understand the technology's capabilities and limitations.

Collaboration between the AI community, regulatory bodies, and ethical organizations is equally crucial. Policymakers must work alongside developers to create frameworks that ensure AI is used responsibly while still enabling innovation. This includes establishing standards for data privacy, fairness, and accountability, as well as mechanisms for auditing AI applications to detect and mitigate misuse.

Ultimately, the release of advanced multimodal AI like NVM 1.0 underscores both the incredible potential and the significant responsibility that comes with such technology. As AI continues to evolve, it is critical to prioritize ethical considerations at every stage of its development and deployment. By addressing these challenges proactively, the AI community can help ensure that these powerful tools are used to empower rather than exploit, driving progress in ways that benefit society as a whole.

Conclusion

NVM 1.0 stands as a defining moment in the evolution of artificial intelligence, a model that has broken free from the traditional boundaries of specialization to excel as a true generalist. By seamlessly bridging the gaps between vision, text, and reasoning tasks, it redefines what is possible in AI. Its ability to integrate these domains without compromise represents a profound shift, demonstrating that advanced multimodal intelligence can be achieved while maintaining exceptional performance in both focused and cross-domain applications.

At its core, NVM 1.0 is not just a technological achievement—it is a tool that democratizes access to the most sophisticated capabilities of AI. By making its model weights and training code openly available, Nvidia has taken a bold step toward leveling the playing field, inviting researchers, startups, and organizations from across the world to participate in shaping the future of AI. This decision doesn't just remove barriers; it accelerates innovation, creating an ecosystem where talent, creativity, and collaboration can thrive.

The model also sets new benchmarks that competitors and future AI systems will strive to match. Whether in healthcare, finance, education, or content creation, NVM 1.0's versatility and precision have demonstrated its ability to transform industries. Its consistent excellence in multimodal tasks and text-based reasoning has laid the groundwork for a new generation of AI models that are not limited by the trade-offs of their predecessors.

Looking forward, NVM 1.0 is more than just a glimpse into the future of AI—it is a blueprint for what is to come. Its hybrid architecture, focus on quality over quantity in training data, and commitment to open-source accessibility are likely to influence the next wave of AI development. It offers a vision of AI that is not just about raw computational power but about thoughtful design, adaptability, and the ability to solve real-world problems in meaningful ways.

Imagine a world where AI systems like NVM 1.0 become ubiquitous, seamlessly integrated into our daily lives. From personalized education platforms to life-saving medical diagnostics, from automating complex workflows to powering creative endeavors, these models could reshape how we interact with technology and with one another. The possibilities are as vast as they are exciting.

As we reflect on the groundbreaking nature of NVM 1.0, it is clear that this is not the end of the story but the beginning of a new chapter in AI innovation. It is a reminder of what can be achieved when ambition meets ingenuity and when technology is shared for the greater good. The world shaped by accessible, versatile, and groundbreaking AI models like NVM 1.0 is a world full of promise—one where progress is no longer confined to a select few but is a shared journey toward a brighter future.

www.ingramcontent.com/pod-product-compliance
Lightning Source LLC
LaVergne TN
LVHW051706050326
832903LV00032B/4041